To obtain more information or to order
copies of *Ocean Waves and Other Tales*,
please contact:

AK Classics
P.O. Box 77203
Charlotte, NC 28271
www.akclassicstories.com
www.oceanwavesandothertales.com
info@oceanwavesandothertales.com

Ocean Waves and Other Tales
Text copyright © 2007 by Helen H. Kimbrough
Illustrations copyright © 2007 by Helen H. Kimbrough
Music copyright © 2007 by Helen H. Kimbrough

Library of Congress
Published by AK Classics
HARDCASE
ISBN-13: 978-0-9814945-0-0
ISBN-10: 0-9814945-0-1
PAPERBACK
ISBN-13: 978-0-9814945-1-7
ISBN-10: 0-9814945-1-x

Illustrations by Lena Shiffman
Music Arranged by D.J. Boyd
Design by Rick Daniel

Printed in the U.S.A.

Ocean Waves
and Other Tales

By Helen H. Kimbrough

Illustrated by Lena Shiffman

Music Arranged by D.J. Boyd

Ocean Waves

I dreamed all night
And wished all day
Of Ocean Waves.

Moving here and moving there
Circling tides and water
everywhere.

Ocean Waves... Ocean Waves... Ocean Waves
Ocean Waves... Ocean Waves... Ocean Waves

In the morning, I got a chance
To play in ocean waves.

Swimming here
And swimming there
Splashing water everywhere.

Ocean Waves... Ocean Waves... Ocean Waves
Ocean Waves... Ocean Waves... Ocean Waves

The next day, I built sand castles
Near the ocean waves.

Scooping here
And scooping there
Building sand castles everywhere.

Ocean Waves... Ocean Waves... Ocean Waves
Ocean Waves... Ocean Waves... Ocean Waves

I am Loved

My mommy feeds me.
My daddy bathes me.

My brother hugs me.
My sister kisses me.

I am loved.
Oh, I am loved.
Oh, I am loved.

My mom packs my lunch.
My dad drives me to school.

My brother wrestles me to the floor.
My sister thinks I'm really cool.

I am loved.
Oh, I am loved.
Oh, I am loved.
Oh, I am loved.

Baby Bear

Baby bear, baby bear
Spin around.

Baby bear, baby bear
Look all around.

Baby bear, baby bear
Peak-a-boo.

Baby bear, baby bear
I see you.

Baby bear, baby bear
Let's jump up and down.

Baby bear, baby bear
Be silly as clowns.

Baby bear, baby bear
God bless you!

Baby bear, baby bear
I love you!

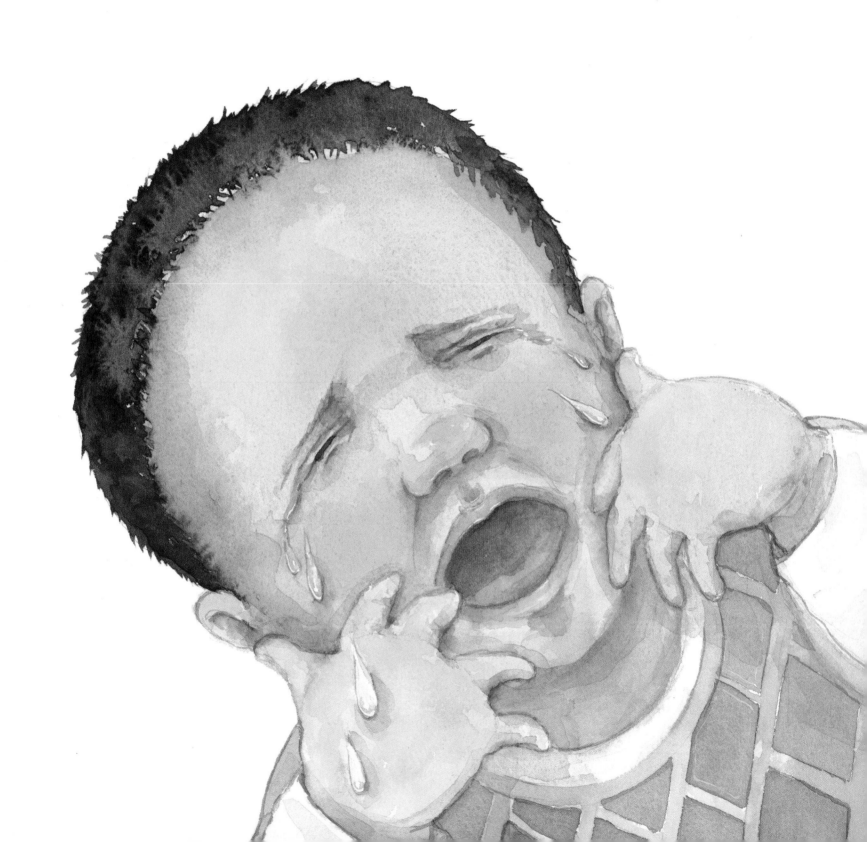

I'm Sleepy

My eyes are getting droopy
I scream for my milk,
My yawn says I'm tired
Please help me get to sleep.

My bath calms and soothes me
My nighttime book amuses me,
My blankie surrounds me
Bedtime is what I need.

I'm sleepy
I'm sleepy
Mommy, I'm sleepy.

I'm sleepy
I'm sleepy
Daddy, I'm sleepy.

I'm sleepy
I'm sleepy
Brother, I'm sleepy.

I'm sleepy
I'm sleepy
Sister, I'm sleepy.

Goodnight!